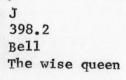

EDITOR'S NOTE:
THE WISE QUEEN is an adaption of a traditional European folktale.
Erika Tachihara retold it in Japanese for the original edition
with these illustrations, based on a version collected by Moses Gaster (1856-1939).
A more common version frequently called "The Clever Peasant Girl" is cited by
Stith Thompson (THE FOLKTALE, University of California Press, 1977).
The story has been retold in English for this edition by Anthea Bell.

Illustrations copyright © 1984, Takeshi Matsumoto
English edition rights arranged by Kodansha Ltd., Tokyo.
English text copyright © 1986, Neugebauer Press USA Inc.
Published in USA by Picture Book Studio USA,
an imprint of Neugebauer Press USA, Inc.
Distributed by Alphabet Press, Natick, MA.
Distributed in Canada by Vanwell Publishing, St. Catharines.
Published in U.K. by Neugebauer Press Publishing Ltd., London.
All rights reserved.
Printed in Austria.

LIBRARY OF CONGRESS CATALOGING IN PUBLICATION DATA

Bell, Anthea.
The wise queen

Summary: A girl's cleverness helps her not only to become the queen,
but to keep that position as well.
[1. Fairy tales. 2. Folklore] I. Iwasaki, Chihiro, 1918-1974, ill. II. Title.
PZ8.B399Wi 1986   398.2'2 [398.2]   [E]   85-29845
ISBN 0-88708-014-6

Ask your bookseller for these other PICTURE BOOK STUDIO books
illustrated by Chihiro Iwasaki:
THE RED SHOES by Hans Christian Andersen
THE LITTLE MERMAID by Hans Christian Andersen
SNOW WHITE AND THE SEVEN DWARVES by The Brothers Grimm

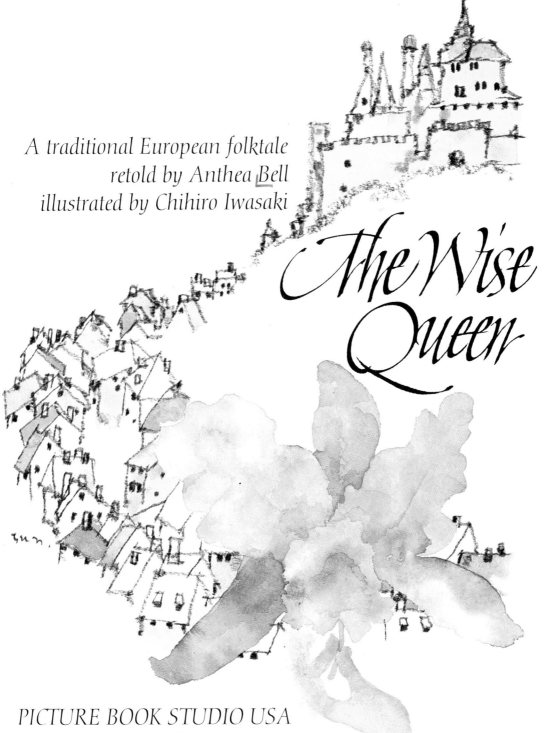

A traditional European folktale
retold by Anthea Bell
illustrated by Chihiro Iwasaki

The Wise Queen

PICTURE BOOK STUDIO USA
Neugebauer Press, London

Once upon a time there was a King who sent for his Minister one day. "I want you to go to market and sell two thousand of my sheep," said the King, "and you must bring me back the sheep as well as the price you're paid for them."

The poor Minister was at his wits' end. "How can I possibly bring the sheep back as well as the money I get for them?" he wondered.

However, the Minister had a clever daughter. When she heard of the task he had to perform, she said, "You must take the sheep to market, shear them and sell their fleeces. Then you can bring the sheep themselves back as well as the money for their wool."

The Minister followed his daughter's advice, took the sheep
to market and brought them home together with the price
he was paid for their fleeces.
"You have done well," the King told him, smiling,
"and I will reward you!"
"My daughter ought to have the reward," said the Minister.
"It was she who told me how to bring back the sheep
as well as the price I was paid for them."
"Your daughter sounds like a clever girl," said the King.
"I should like to meet her." And he told his Minister,
"Send her to the palace clothed, yet naked,
and neither riding nor walking."
What was the Minister to do now?

Once again his daughter solved the problem.
She took off her clothes and wrapped
herself in a net instead, and she mounted
a donkey so small that her feet brushed
the ground as it went along.
So she was able to go to the palace clothed yet naked,
and neither walking nor riding.

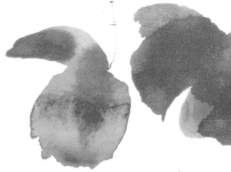

The King was pleased.
"The Minister's daughter certainly is a very
clever girl," he thought, and he decided
to marry her.

So the two of them were married, but after the wedding the King told his Queen, "You must promise me one thing: never interfere with my decisions in the court of law."

One day the girl who was now Queen saw a boy walking along the road, weeping bitterly.

"What is the matter?" she asked.

"Oh," said the boy, through his tears, "my calf has been taken away. My own cow bore that calf, but a man went to the King and claimed that his horse gave birth to it, and when the case came to trial the King believed him."

"Ask for another trial," said the Queen, "and do as I will tell you."

So next day the boy went to the court of law, and told the King,
"A carp jumped out of the water and ate my sheep alive."
The King was astonished. "How can such a strange thing be?" he asked.
"Why," said the boy, "it's no stranger than to hear of a horse giving
birth to a calf."

"You are quite right," said the King, "and I see I made the wrong decision yesterday. That calf must be yours after all."
The boy was delighted. "Now I'll get my calf back, and all thanks to the Queen!" he cried.

The King was furious when he heard this.
"You have broken your promise and interfered with my decisions
in the court of law," he told the Queen. "You must leave my palace."
"Very well," said the Queen. "I will go, but first, may I entertain you
to a banquet for the last time?"

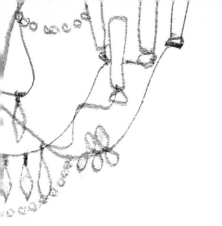

So she held a banquet, and during the feasting she turned to the King and said, "My lord, I ask you to grant me one wish.
When I leave your palace, let me take one thing home with me, the thing I love most."
"Very well," said the King, "you may take the thing you love most, but nothing else."
After that the King had a great deal to eat and drink and soon fell fast asleep.

The Queen put him into a
carriage and took him home
to her father's house.

Next morning, waking in a strange place, the King looked around him in amazement.

"Why have you brought me here?" he asked the Queen.

"Didn't you say I could take the thing I loved most home with me when I left the palace?" asked the Queen, smiling.

"How clever you are," said the King, "and how loving! I have been in the wrong. Stay with me and be my wife for always."

And ever afterwards, the King consulted his Queen in all his decisions.